A Trainer's Manual
for Process Politics

A Trainer's Manual for Process Politics

Eileen Guthrie
Warren Sam Miller
William Grimberg

University Associates, Inc.
8517 Production Avenue
P.O. Box 26240
San Diego, CA 92126

PREFACE

This trainer's manual is designed as a resource to use with *Process Politics: A Guide for Group Leaders* in a group-facilitation setting. Although the manual is intended for trainers with previous experience, it may be useful to less-experienced trainers as an introduction to designing and facilitating. It is assumed that the trainer will become thoroughly familiar with the contents of the guide and the authors' approaches to the material. It is also suggested that each participant attending a training session read the guide in advance and have a copy of it for use during the session.

It is helpful to view this manual as a beginning for developing one's own methods and structures for teaching process politics. Some of the best learning comes from the participants themselves. It is important to pay explicit attention to the participants' individual and collective self-interests, styles, and interactions. Above all, the manual should be used as a way to increase opportunities for the trainer and the participants to become acquainted and have fun while learning together.

We particularly want to thank Carol Nolde for her editorial assistance, as well as Betty Aldridge, Susan Conway Grimberg, and Danny Collard for their personal support during our work on this project.

It is our hope that you will enjoy the time you spend with both the guide and the manual. Your comments and reactions would be appreciated.

Eileen Guthrie   Warren Sam Miller
2412 First Avenue South   124 Valley High Road
Minneapolis, Minnesota 55404   Burnsville, Minnesota 55337

William Grimberg
1220 Union Commerce Building
Cleveland, Ohio 44115

August, 1981

CONTENTS

PART I

Part I provides a discussion of the trainer's role, including such topics as the principles of trainer conduct, training techniques, responsibilities, stylistic considerations, and the importance of using evaluation in a workshop setting. In addition, it presents information about planning and preparatory work that must be completed prior to conducting the training experience and a specific workshop structure as well as variations of that structure.

THE TRAINER'S ROLE

The goal of training in process politics is to help the participants become more effective as members of groups. Effectiveness as a group member requires more than knowledge of the dynamics of change and group process; it requires an understanding of one's own feelings, motivations, and behaviors as well as a clear perspective of their impact in a variety of group situations. Conceptual and theoretical principles can be most helpful when they are presented in a way that enables the participants to be aware of alternative behaviors and to choose those that are most effective in different situations.

Activity designs in this manual are based on a "do-look-learn" approach to helping the participants learn the concepts and skills discussed in the guide. This approach encourages the participants to share experiences focused on particular learning objectives. It relies on participant knowledge as the basis for learning, whether that knowledge is gained in group sessions or drawn from prior experiences. The participant interactions involved in the training activities provide an opportunity to produce behavioral and self-awareness data that can be examined in terms of its impact on the group and its aims.

The "do-look-learn" model can be summarized as follows:

1. *Do* an activity that enables the participants to try new behaviors or to think about their typical styles of behavior.

2. *Look* at the activity in terms of the feelings and reactions of the participants. This stage of the training process helps the participants understand the impact of their behaviors on themselves and on the functioning of the group.

3. *Learn* from the activity and the discussion that follows. The group's experience and its impact are evaluated in light of the goals stated in the design. The participants generalize from the activity by examining why certain behaviors work better than others in various situations.

By using the "do-look-learn" model, the trainer can create worthwhile learning opportunities for the participants.

PRINCIPLES OF TRAINER CONDUCT

By making active use of the basic communication skills outlined in the guide, the trainer can facilitate interactions within the group. In addition, adhering to the following principles of conduct can be of value to the trainer:

1. *Speak from personal experience.* When the participants ask questions about the "right" answer in a given situation or challenge the trainer's interpretation of a concept, the trainer's best response is to talk about his or her own experience. In this way the trap of power struggles can be avoided, and the participants will expand their perspectives about what is possible. Speaking for oneself also underscores the importance of other principles presented in the guide, such as learning from doing, considering many approaches to change, and so forth. (See Chapter 1 in the guide.)

2. *Use feedback properly.* Feedback must be accepted as well as offered, must be nonjudgmental and descriptive, and must offer a way to change if appropriate. The trainer should follow the guidelines for effective feedback while facilitating the participants' active learning of those guidelines. (See Chapter 7 in the guide.)

3. *Keep the activities moving.* It is important to keep track of the time allotted; to announce shifts; and, if appropriate, to give a two-minute signal before concluding. The participants may resist time limits, especially during activities in which they are to complete a task. Under these circumstances it is useful to remind them that actually finishing the task is not as important as learning from the process data that have already been generated.

4. *Provide short summaries as transitions.* When beginning a session, the trainer should share the agenda with the participants as an overview of what will take place during the time available. When moving from one section of the agenda to another, it is a good idea to take some time to summarize what has just transpired and what the group will be doing next. The agenda should be somewhat flexible, however, to allow time to pursue valuable learning experiences generated by the participants themselves.

TRAINING TECHNIQUES

Lecturing

In using the guide, it is valuable to present material in a lecture format in two situations: when introducing concepts and specific skills and when summarizing the major points that have arisen during an activity.

One suggestion is to *keep lectures short.* Participants generally learn more about a concept or skill by practicing or experiencing it than by hearing about it. Furthermore, many of the concepts in the guide may appear confusing at first, and many questions may occur to the participants as they attempt to interpret those concepts. Rather than spend time theorizing and responding to abstract questions, the trainer should provide a concise introduction to a concept and then progress to an activity that highlights that concept in practice.

Another way to increase the usefulness of short lectures is to *use examples,* preferably from personal experience, as a way of enabling the participants to translate principles into useful tools. This approach also provides information about the trainer that the participants may find interesting.

Sometimes participants argue about a point, questioning its validity, its usefulness, or the trainer's interpretation. For example, this may occur after an activity that has not gone well or after the participants have had difficulty with an activity. In such cases it is best to avoid power struggles over the issue and state that although some people may not find an idea useful, others may benefit from it. If the situation calls for further attention, it is valuable to concentrate on turning the discussion into a learning experience for everyone.

Consulting

The "do-look-learn" theory can also be applied by participants in their involvements outside the training sessions as members of clubs, cooperatives, community organizations, or work groups. These involvements can prove invaluable as settings for the application of process politics.

There are several ways to provide the participants with opportunities to help each other apply their learnings to their outside involvements. One approach is to plan for open-agenda time at each session for *participant-to-participant* consultation. The participants are allowed a block of time to request help from the group on particular situations in which they are involved and thereby obtain practical consultation assistance, practice in describing group situations, and demonstrations of the value of third-party consultation. This can be done with the total group or with a group-on-group arrangement in the center of the room in which the person requesting help caucuses with several others as the rest of the participants observe the consulting process and offer feedback on what they see.

Trainer-to-participant consultation is another alternative. The participants expect practical advice from the trainer, and it is useful to provide such advice during or between sessions. This practice not only allows further amplification of the concepts and skills of process politics but also provides the participants with individual attention.

Finally, *participant-to-trainer* consultation can be of value. For example, the trainer can either present a case study with which he or she needs help or encourage the participants to formally evaluate the level and quality of training provided. In either case the participants are given an opportunity to practice drawing on their own knowledge.

Developing a Case Study

As mentioned previously, the trainer's own experience can be a useful tool in conducting process-politics training. Presenting an effective case study is one way of conveying such experience.

A case study, whether real or fictitious, must first *describe a specific group*. The trainer must clarify the group's size, its primary purpose, and how it came to exist. The next step is to *develop a summarizing statement* about the dynamics of the group. Describing the situation, those who are affected by the situation, possible causes of problems, and organizational strengths and weaknesses can highlight the way in which a group is functioning. It is also essential that the trainer *define his or her relationship and commitment* to the group. In a fictitious case, for example, the trainer might decide to be a member of an organization's board of directors. This information reflects the trainer's commitment to the group as well as his or her ability and desire to effect change.

Finally, the trainer must *describe the resources available* so that any gaps in both talents and resources become apparent.

Employing Guided Fantasy and Role Playing

Guided-fantasy and role-play techniques are especially appropriate when the trainer wishes to have the participants focus on a specific issue or identify with a certain situation (such as one of those presented as examples in the guide).

Guided fantasy is a technique for helping people to generate images, sounds, and situations in a fantasy state of consciousness. To conduct a guided fantasy, the trainer should encourage the participants to make themselves comfortable by taking off their shoes, sitting on the floor, or whatever seems appropriate. Sometimes it is helpful to dim the lights to encourage a relaxed, meditative atmosphere.

Before leading the participants through a specific sequence of suggestions or instructions to stimulate their fantasies, the trainer should ensure their relaxation by suggesting in a low, rhythmic voice that they relax one part of their bodies at a time while breathing evenly and regularly. After several minutes of systematic relaxation suggestions, the guided fantasy can be begun. After it has been completed, the participants should be allowed ample time to leave the fantasy and to reorient themselves.

Role playing is another effective technique for generating ex-periential-learning situations.[1] Before beginning the role play, the trainer should give the participants time to think privately about and assume the characteristics of their roles. The trainer also needs to pay special attention to helping the participants unwind and talk about their role-play experience after it has ended. It is possible for such an experience to become very intense, and the participants may identify aspects of themselves that they wish to spend time exploring further. Thus, they must be given an opportunity to talk together or to seek personal time with the trainer.

THE TRAINER'S RESPONSIBILITIES

It is important to remember that the trainer bears the ultimate responsibility for the overall organization of sessions; for facilitation during individual sessions; and for helping the participants extract specific, practical learnings.

---

[1] For further information on this technique, refer to N.R.F. Maier, A.R. Solem, and A.A. Maier, *The Role-Play Technique: A Handbook for Management and Leadership Practice*, University Associates, 1975.

Essentially, the trainer is a "learning facilitator." By acknowledging and calling on the resources of the entire group, the trainer ensures that everyone becomes part of the learning experience. Responsibility and ownership of the learning process can be rotated, the curriculum can be modified and evolved, and the participants can be given the opportunity to learn more about themselves. By using real-life data, the participants can help each other not only identify personal expertise but also acknowledge it, integrate it, and learn to use it.

THE TRAINER'S STYLE

The most effective way to conduct process-politics training is to build and learn from the group's own processes. This calls for a style that is flexible, with a premium placed on interactions between participants as opposed to a format relying primarily on lectures.

There are several specific ways in which the trainer can facilitate learning about group processes:

1. *Avoid jargon* unless it is carefully explained.

2. *Exemplify the principles of process politics.* For example, when emphasizing the importance of paying attention to both task and maintenance functions in a group, it is essential to pay explicit attention to those dimensions within the present learning group.

3. *Draw on actual situations* in which the participants are involved. This practice increases their investment in the learning process and provides assistance that often turns out to be of immediate use to the participants outside the group.

4. *Use a variety of process-observation approaches.* For many participants, learning how to observe a group in action is a key to increased awareness about ways to help groups become more effective. Thus, the participants should be encouraged to provide each other and the trainer with feedback and consultation and to talk with each other about an activity after its completion, whether formally during the session or informally during breaks, over the phone, or at a local cafe. An option is to rotate the position of process observer with each session and to focus on a different aspect of group dynamics each time.

5. *Let the participants know that their ideas, criticisms, and comments are valued.* Acknowledge and build on differences.

6. *Emphasize positive feedback.* The trainer who consciously focuses on reinforcement of what the participants are doing "right"

encourages them to take greater risks, thereby increasing their possibilities for learning. Making positive feedback statements also provides the participants with the ability to build on existing skills and to identify changes they wish to make or new skills they wish to learn.

EVALUATION: AN ONGOING PROCESS

As stated earlier, evaluation is a key element in process politics. It is also important to the success of any workshop or session. Ongoing, effective evaluation produces both process and content data relevant to the subjects being presented. Evaluation during a session (also called *processing*) can help the trainer identify issues and skills of particular interest or concern to the participants so that they can be emphasized during the remainder of the session. The maintenance checks in the Appendix of the guide can be useful tools for evaluation.

Another approach to evaluating a session consists of allowing time for personal reflection. Possible questions for each participant's consideration include the following: "How comfortable am I in the group, and how am I able to express my feelings? What satisfactions do I derive from my behavior, and how might I handle myself differently? What are the most significant things that are happening in the group? What is causing these things to happen, and how have I influenced their occurrence? To what extent am I obtaining what I want from this session?"

It is best to keep evaluations simple. The reason for evaluating, as previously explained, is to generate data that can be used either in the remainder of a session or at a later date. Sometimes taking a quick poll of the participants regarding what they have liked, disliked, and learned is enough to keep a session on track for meeting the participants' needs or determining the effectiveness of a particular design.

The trainer should be creative in approaches to evaluations. The method used at any given time should be specific to the situation involved; it is up to the trainer to be aware of what is happening in a session and to use an appropriate method of evaluation. For example, simply asking in the middle of a discussion whether the participants are finding the discussion useful allows the trainer to determine whether to continue. On the other hand, a simple evaluation may not be enough if the trainer senses a great deal of dissatisfaction within the group. Serious discontent is a good indication that a more detailed questionnaire or interview process that facilitates greater group involvement would be appropriate.

CONCLUSION

The comments and suggestions offered in this chapter are drawn from the authors' experiences in presenting the concepts and skills developed in the guide. They are designed to be stimulants to the trainer's thinking as he or she develops a training curriculum. The trainer should feel free to adapt the following materials as necessary, to share ideas with others in the field, and to take time to learn from the training process.

WORKSHOP PLANNING AND EXECUTION

THE TRAINER'S PREWORK

Before offering and conducting a training workshop, it is necessary to consider a number of factors. The trainer first must determine the intent of the training and for whom it has been designed. The next step is to make some determinations about the participant group by answering the following questions: Are the participants already acquainted with each other? Are they from the same system or different systems? What are their mutual and individual concerns? Which of these concerns can be met through this particular training?

The physical setting and materials required must also be considered. Such matters as room size; furniture requirements; and the availability of supplies like a chalkboard and chalk (or newsprint and felt-tipped markers), handouts, blank paper, and pencils or pens are not difficult to arrange with a little forethought. Failure to address these logistical issues, however, can seriously impair the effectiveness of even the most experienced trainer.

Finally, the trainer should estimate the time and money that will go into the training. Issues to consider are the amount of time available; the amount of time that the trainer and participants want to devote to various topics; the cost of attending the training; and how much the trainer will be paid, if at all.

Many other significant issues relevant to a particular training situation must be taken into account before the workshop can take place. The foregoing considerations are simply starting points for planning any type of training.

WORKSHOP STRUCTURE

The suggested workshop structure includes all of the activity designs presented in this manual. It is divided into twelve sessions; each of the first eleven is approximately two to three hours in duration, and the final session lasts one hour. The sessions can be scheduled on consecutive days, excluding evenings; in a residential setting with three sessions per day, including evenings; or in any combination of daytime and evening sessions that is convenient for all concerned.

The recommended sequence of sessions is as follows:

Session One (three hours)

Who We Are: A Getting-Acquainted Activity (fifty minutes)

How Groups Interact: A Simulation (one hour and twenty-five minutes)

Group Memberships: Taking Inventory (forty-five minutes)

Session Two (two hours and fifteen minutes)

Change: How to Live with It (one hour and twenty minutes)

Roles of the Process Politician: Assessing Effectiveness (fifty-five minutes)

Session Three (two hours and forty minutes)

Making the Most of Personal Energy (fifty-five minutes)

Determining Life Chapters (forty-five minutes)

Feedback: Principles and Practice (one hour)

Session Four (two hours and thirty-five minutes)

Using Personal Power: A Fantasy Experience (one hour)

Identifying Personal Support Groups (one hour)

Role Models: Teaching and Learning Relationships (thirty-five minutes)

Session Five (two hours and fifty-five minutes)

Taking Care of Oneself: Remedies for Burnout (one and one-half hours)

Basic Group Dynamics: An Interaction (one hour and twenty-five minutes)

Session Six (two hours and fifteen minutes)

Leadership Styles: A Personal Assessment

Session Seven (two hours and twenty minutes)

Action Planning and Evaluation

Session Eight (two and one-half hours)

Positive Thinking: Planning for Success (one hour and fifteen minutes)

Effective Communication: Learning Basic Skills (one hour and fifteen minutes)

Session Nine (two hours and twenty-five minutes)

Successful Meetings: Clarifying and Evaluating (one hour and twenty-five minutes)

Behind the Scenes: Examining Informal Group Activities (thirty minutes)

Group Consultants: Identifying Valuable Nonmembers (thirty minutes)

Session Ten (three hours and five minutes)

Conflict Resolution: An Overview (one hour)

"Last-Ditch" Strategies: A Brainstorming Activity (one hour)

Building a System Mobile (one hour and five minutes)

Session Eleven (two hours)

Institutional Values: A Role-Play Activity

Session Twelve (one hour)

Magic Wand: Personal Action Planning

VARIATIONS

In many instances the subject matter of a workshop is predetermined, as in the preceding workshop design. In some situations, however, only broad topics such as "organization development" or "group dynamics" are announced. In these cases the trainer may wish to outline specific subjects with which he or she is prepared to deal and request that the participants assist in determining the priorities of each session. Many of the activity designs in this manual may be adapted to meet such a need for flexibility.

Another way to meet a need for flexibility is to construct a one-to three-day workshop by selecting and combining a few of the previously listed activities or sessions. This alternative is appropriate when a weekend event is scheduled, for instance. Such workshops of shorter duration often appeal to people who are members of an ongoing group or of similar groups.

In sessions in which the participants do not know each other, it is important to recognize their need to make contact with each other on a personal level and to relax and enjoy themselves. If strangers are to spend up to three days together, it is advisable to devote considerably more time to getting-acquainted activities than might normally be the case with ongoing groups.

PART II

Part II consists of twenty-five activity designs that accompany the material presented in the guide. Suitable for use with groups of all types, these activities are derived from the authors' experiences as group developers and trainers in a variety of settings from inner-city neighborhoods to large corporations. The purpose of these activities is to teach the skills that an individual needs to become a successful process politician and to be able to foster group effectiveness. Participants are given the opportunity to learn new skills, sharpen old skills, and gain new conceptual understandings of the ways in which groups operate. Also, with support and assistance from the trainer and each other, participants can gain awareness of their own particular group settings.

WHO WE ARE: A GETTING-ACQUAINTED ACTIVITY

Goals

I. To give the participants a chance to meet each other.

II. To generate data about the interests of the participants and their expectations for the workshop.

III. To encourage group interaction.

Group Size

Flexible.

Time Required

Fifty minutes.

Physical Setting

A room large enough to accommodate subgroups. Seating should be flexible.

Materials

I. Sets of newsprint signs to post on the walls (prepared by the trainer prior to the activity).

1. Sign Set Number 1 (types of places in which the participants grew up):
   a. Suburb
   b. City
   c. Town
   d. Rural Environment

2. Sign Set Number 2 (the participants' responses to the idea of change):
   a. I become afraid when I think about change.
   b. Change occurs rapidly and is out of my control, so I just accept it.
   c. Things are fine the way they are.
   d. Change happens too slowly to suit me.

    3. Sign Set Number 3 (the participants' expectations for the workshop):

        a. I want some help on problems that I am having with group activities.

        b. I am mainly interested in what the trainer can teach me.

        c. I want to make contact with new people.

        d. I want to learn something new.

II. Masking tape to use in posting signs.

III. Blank paper for each recorder.

IV. A pencil or pen for each recorder.

V. A clipboard or other portable writing surface for each recorder.

Procedure

I. *(Five minutes.)* The trainer introduces the activity and its goals.

II. *(Ten minutes.)* After posting the four signs of Sign Set Number 1, the trainer instructs each participant to move to the sign that best fits the type of place in which he or she grew up. The participants grouped by each sign are asked to form triads to talk about their reactions to the environments in which they grew up.

III. *(Ten minutes.)* The first set of signs is removed, and the four signs of Sign Set Number 2 are posted. Each participant is instructed to move to the sign that best describes his or her current attitude about change. The participants grouped by each sign form dyads and interview each other to find out about their experiences with change in their lives.

IV. *(Ten minutes.)* The second set of signs is removed, and the fours signs of Sign Set Number 3 are posted. Each participant is asked to move to the sign that best describes his or her expectations for the workshop. The participants grouped by each sign are asked to appoint a recorder. Each recorder is given blank paper, a pencil or pen, and a clipboard or other portable writing surface and is asked to makes notes as the members of his or her subgroup discuss the following:

    1. The types of problems they are currently experiencing with group activities;

    2. Any additional information they would like to have about the trainer;

3. The types of people they would like to meet during the workshop; and

4. The subjects about which they would like to learn during the workshop.

V. *(Ten minutes.)* The total group is reconvened, and each sub-group recorder shares the content of the notes taken during step IV. Additional concerns and expectations are discussed if time permits.

VI. *(Five minutes.)* The entire experience is discussed and evaluated.

Variation

Instead of using Sign Set Number 3, the trainer may reassemble the total group for a general discussion of the participants' attitudes toward change. (Refer to Change: Framework for Action in Chapter 1 of the guide.)

HOW GROUPS INTERACT: A SIMULATION

Goals

I. To provide the participants with an experience in the multi-faceted nature of a typical organizational issue.

II. To encourage group interaction.

III. To demonstrate that what is "right" and what is "wrong" are largely matters of one's perspective in a situation.

IV. To help the participants gain an understanding of the ways in which individual and subgroup self-interests influence group effectiveness.

Group Size

At least twelve participants.

Time Required

One hour and twenty-five minutes.

Physical Setting

A room large enough to accommodate four separate subgroups. Seating should be flexible.

Materials

I. A copy of the Case-Situation Handout for each participant.

II. Enough copies of the School-Board Member Role Description to distribute to all members of the school-board subgroup.

III. Enough copies of the Parent Role Description to distribute to all members of the parent subgroup.

IV. Enough copies of the Teachers' Union Member Role Description to distribute to all members of the teachers' union subgroup.

V. Enough copies of the Community-Organization Member Role Description to distribute to all members of the community-organization subgroup.

Procedure

I. *(Five minutes.)* The trainer introduces the activity and its goals, indicating that each participant will be asked to play a role.

II. *(Ten minutes.)* Each participant is given a copy of the Case-Situation Handout and is asked to read this handout silently.

III. *(Five minutes.)* The participants are divided into four sub- groups of similar size: the *school-board subgroup*, the *parent subgroup*, the *teachers' union subgroup*, and the *community-organization subgroup*. Each participant then receives a copy of the role description for his or her subgroup.

IV. *(Ten minutes.)* The trainer requests that the subgroups meet separately. The members of each subgroup read and study the assigned role description and then discuss ideas about the situation as well as a strategy for the community meeting.

V. *(Thirty minutes.)* The subgroups conduct a community meeting to discuss the issues presented in the Case-Situation Handout.

VI. *(Ten minutes.)* After thirty minutes the trainer stops the community meeting; reconvenes the total group; and leads a discussion of the experience, integrating the material on self-interest from The Individual and The Contexts in Which We Live in Chapter 3 of the guide.

VII. *(Ten minutes.)* The trainer discusses The Importance of Groups in Managing Change and Process Politics: The Art of the Possible from Chapter 1 of the guide.

VIII. *(Five minutes.)* The total group evaluates the experience, paying particular attention to unresolved feelings generated by the role play.

Variation

The trainer may substitute a different case situation and accompanying role descriptions if desired. Any situation chosen should be one that the participants can identify with easily and one that offers several different options as solutions to the problem presented.

Remarks

The participants should be reminded at the conclusion of the role play that they need not worry about leaving their discussion unfinished; however, they should also be helped to defuse their leftover feelings. (Refer to the "do-look-learn" model in the chapter on The Trainer's Role.)

Case-Situation Handout

Central Elementary School has been the neighborhood grade school and a community fixture for as long as anyone can remember. One reason for pride in the school is that in recent years it has become naturally and easily integrated without busing or fanfare. In this respect the school is a reflection of Central Neighborhood.

The school board, faced with declining enrollment, court-ordered desegregation, inflation, and budget deficits, has decided that Central is to be one of five grade schools to be closed next year. Two hundred teaching positions in the school system are to be eliminated as well. The teachers have responded by questioning what is happening to the quality of education. The parents cannot imagine life without a community school, and the local community organization wonders about the intelligence of a school board that closes a naturally integrated school when one of its major problems is how to desegregate.

The immediate situation is a neighborhood meeting at the school two weeks after the school-board decision. Four groups are represented at the meeting:

1. the school board
2. parents
3. the teachers' union
4. the community organization

School-Board Member
Role Description

You are a member of the school board. You like the idea of neighborhood schools, especially at the elementary level, and you struggled with the decision to close Central. The overall decrease in student population has resulted in declining revenues, and at the same time inflationary pressures have increased costs rapidly. The Central building is old, making upkeep and energy costs higher than those for some of the more modern facilities that will be kept open. You voted to close Central in spite of the fact that the neighborhood is stable and naturally integrated. The economics were just too convincing to do otherwise.

Parent Role Description

You are the parent of two children who attend Central Elementary School. You like the fact that your children can attend school in their own neighborhood; they can walk to and from school safely and easily, and you are able to maintain close contact with the faculty and staff.

You are not opposed to racial integration, but you strongly dislike the idea that your children will be bused to school for any reason. In fact, you selected and moved to this area several years ago largely because of the proximity of Central. You are angry about the school board's decision to close this school.

Teachers' Union Member
Role Description

You are an active member of the teachers' union. Your primary concern is lack of job security due to the fact that teaching positions have been eliminated for the past two years and are now being eliminated for the coming year as well. You are tired of seeing good teachers leave the field because of this insecurity and you wonder about the school board's decision to reduce the number of teaching positions rather than to eliminate certain administrative and other nonteaching jobs. In addition, although you are active in a movement to improve the quality of education by reducing class size, you see that classes are growing larger. You have serious questions about the intelligence and motives of school-board members.

Community-Organization Member
Role Description

You are active in the Central Neighborhood Community Organization. Although your own children no longer attend Central Elementary School, you are concerned about the impact that the closing of the school might have on local property values. One of the major factors that affected your decision to move to this neighborhood was the nearby school, and you have heard several other residents express the same motivation. Because you feel certain that the lack of a neighborhood school will adversely affect the value of local property, you are prepared to go to court if necessary to keep Central open.

GROUP MEMBERSHIPS: TAKING INVENTORY

Goals

I. To demonstrate the concept that a group consists of people who have something in common.

II. To help the participants become more aware of their memberships in various groups.

III. To reveal the different types of things that the participants have in common with each other.

Group Size

Flexible.

Time Required

Forty-five minutes.

Physical Setting

A room with movable chairs to allow the participants to form dyads. Writing surfaces should also be provided.

Materials

I. Group-Affiliation Inventory (guide, p. 5).

II. A pencil or pen for each participant.

Procedure

I. *(Five minutes.)* The trainer introduces the activity by presenting applicable material from The Importance of Groups in Managing Change in Chapter 1 of the guide. The participants are informed that a group is a collection of people who have something in common; examples are mentioned.

II. *(Five minutes.)* The participants are asked to review Chapter 1 in the guide.

III. *(Fifteen minutes.)* The trainer distributes pencils or pens to all participants and asks them to complete the Group-Affiliation

Inventory (guide, p. 5). The participants are also asked to consider which groups they belong to by choice, which they belong to by accident, which memberships they can change, and which memberships they cannot change.

IV. *(Five minutes.)* The participants are instructed to select partners and to share their completed inventories with their partners.

V. *(Fifteen minutes.)* The total group is reconvened and discusses the seven characteristics of groups listed in The Importance of Groups in Managing Change in Chapter 1 of the guide.

Variation

The trainer may focus the activity on other aspects of groups, such as those presented in Phases of Group Development in Chapter 5 of the guide.

CHANGE: HOW TO LIVE WITH IT

Goals

    I. To heighten the participants' awareness of the dynamics of change in a group.

    II. To analyze the ways in which individuals can be affected by group change.

    III. To help the participants become familiar with various tools for managing change.

Group Size

A maximum of thirty participants.

Time Required

One hour and twenty minutes.

Physical Setting

A room large enough to accommodate dyads. Seating should be flexible and comfortable.

Materials

    I. A chalkboard and chalk or newsprint flip charts and felt-tipped markers.

    II. A set of stimulus statements constituting a fantasy experience in which each participant is asked to think about a current or recent change in a group to which he or she belongs. (These statements are prepared by the trainer prior to conducting the activity. They should accommodate both *short-term* changes, such as those in response to a crisis, and *long-term* changes, such as those associated with transition periods or with the gradual termination of a group.)

Procedure

    I. *(Five minutes.)* The trainer introduces the activity and its goals.

II. *(Ten minutes.)* Each participant is asked to become as comfortable and relaxed as possible and to silently reflect on a group to which he or she belongs. The trainer then leads the participants through a fantasy experience involving group change.

III. *(Ten minutes.)* The trainer asks the participants to form pairs and to discuss their attitudes and feelings about the changes experienced. The participants are encouraged to be aware of their physical sensations and to monitor their feelings as they talk about their groups.

IV. *(Ten minutes.)* After reconvening the total group, the trainer asks volunteers to list quickly on a chalkboard or newsprint the feelings they had or the responses they encountered. General discussion follows about the positive and negative aspects of their feelings and responses, whether their feelings and responses affected them only or other members of their groups as well, paradoxes involved with the changes, their degrees of distance from the changes, and so forth.

V. *(Ten minutes.)* The trainer presents the following concepts:

1. Change can be planned for and managed.
2. It is important to become aware of change as a paradox.
3. It is important to monitor personal feelings and energy.

When presenting the third concept, the trainer incorporates material from Change: Framework for Action and Approaches to Change in Chapter 1 of the guide and from How to Make the Most of Personal Energy in Chapter 2 of the guide.

VI. *(Fifteen minutes.)* The participants again form pairs and relate the concepts just presented to their own specific group-change experiences. Each participant concentrates on explaining to his or her partner the exact nature of the change situation, the problem associated with it, and how that problem might be or might have been solved.

VII. *(Fifteen minutes.)* The trainer reconvenes the total group, asks the participants to share the tools they identified for managing change, and augments as necessary.

VIII. *(Five minutes.)* The activity is discussed and evaluated.

ROLES OF THE PROCESS POLITICIAN: ASSESSING EFFECTIVENESS

Goals

I. To examine the various roles of the process politician in different settings.

II. To determine the level of effectiveness and satisfaction experienced by the participants in the roles that they have assumed.

III. To help the participants decide which roles they would like to assume as process politicians.

Group Size

A maximum of thirty participants.

Time Required

Fifty-five minutes.

Physical Setting

A room with flexible seating to accommodate subgroups of two to four participants each.

Materials

A chalkboard and chalk or a newsprint flip chart and a felt-tipped marker (optional).

Procedure

I. *(Ten minutes.)* The trainer introduces the activity, its goals, and the content of Roles of the Process Politician in Chapter 2 of the guide. Highlights may be written on a chalkboard or newsprint if the trainer wishes.

II. *(Five minutes.)* Focusing on the five roles delineated in Chapter 2 of the guide, the trainer asks the participants to silently reflect on the ways in which they have assumed these roles in the past and the settings in which they did so.

III. *(Fifteen minutes.)* The participants are asked to form subgroups of two to four each and to share their views of themselves as process politicians, their assessments of their own effectiveness, and their levels of satisfaction with their experiences in this regard. The trainer encourages the participants to take some risks at self-disclosure while completing this step. As the subgroups proceed, the trainer moves around the room for the purpose of monitoring progress, helping the participants keep to the subject, and offering intervention or support if needed.

IV. *(Fifteen minutes.)* The members of each subgroup are instructed to consider which aspects of their functioning as process politicians they wish to maintain as well as which aspects they wish to change, to share their opinions with their fellow subgroup members, and to seek suggestions for ways to accomplish desired changes.

V. *(Ten minutes.)* The trainer reassembles the total group and leads a discussion on the following subjects:

1. The process-politician roles that have been effective for people in various settings;
2. The changes toward which the participants wish to work;
3. The patterns that emerge from discussion of the first two subjects; and
4. The participants' satisfaction with the activity as well as the learnings derived.

MAKING THE MOST OF PERSONAL ENERGY

Goals

   I. To help the participants identify their own energy resources and depleters.

  II. To present techniques for increasing personal energy.

Group Size

Flexible.

Time Required

Fifty-five minutes.

Physical Setting

A room with flexible seating to allow the participants to form dyads. Writing surfaces should also be provided.

Materials

   I. Energy-Account Work Sheet (guide, p. 28).

  II. A pencil or pen for each participant.

Procedure

   I. *(Five minutes.)* The trainer introduces the activity and its goals, pointing out that an objective measure of energy resources and depleters is not necessary because everyone feels the existence of these elements. It is further emphasized that skills at controlling energy resources can be both learned and strengthened. The trainer refers to material presented in How to Make the Most of Personal Energy in Chapter 2 of the guide.

  II. *(Ten minutes.)* The participants are given pencils or pens and are instructed to complete the Energy-Account Work Sheet (guide, p. 28).

 III. *(Twenty minutes.)* The participants choose partners and discuss and compare their completed work sheets.

IV. *(Fifteen minutes.)* The trainer reconvenes the total group and leads a discussion on the participants' learnings about their own energy.

V. *(Five minutes.)* The experience is discussed and evaluated.

DETERMINING LIFE CHAPTERS

Goals

I. To help the participants identify the developmental phases of their lives.

II. To acquaint the participants with the developmental phases of group life.

Group Size

Flexible.

Time Required

Forty-five minutes.

Physical Setting

A room with movable chairs to accommodate dyads and with writing surfaces for all participants.

Materials

I. Part III of the Self-Analysis Work Sheet (guide, p. 40).

II. A pencil or pen for each participant.

III. Blank paper for each participant.

Procedure

I. *(Five minutes.)* By summarizing material derived from The Individual in Chapter 3 of the guide, the trainer presents the concept of determining one's life chapters. An example is provided, and it is emphasized that the major chapters in a person's life are those that are important to that person.

II. *(Ten minutes.)* After distributing pencils or pens, the trainer asks the participants to complete Part III of the Self-Analysis Work Sheet (guide, p. 40).

III. *(Five minutes.)* The trainer distributes blank paper and requests that the participants list the principal groups to which they belonged during each of the chapters in their lives.

IV. *(Ten minutes.)* The participants form dyads, share the lists completed in steps II and III, and describe to each other the main characteristics of their life chapters.

V. *(Ten minutes.)* The trainer reconvenes the total group and asks the participants to share their learnings about themselves or the groups to which they have belonged. During the course of the sharing, the trainer incorporates relevant information from Phases of Group Development in Chapter 5 of the guide. Parallels are drawn between individual development and group development.

VI. *(Five minutes.)* The activity is discussed and evaluated.

Variations

I. If sufficient time is available and the trainer wishes to delve more deeply into the role of self-awareness in process politics, the participants may be asked to complete and discuss the rest of the Self-Analysis Work Sheet, the Value-Clarification Work Sheet, and the Activity/Payoff Analysis, all of which appear in Chapter 3 of the guide.

II. The trainer may focus solely on group development as discussed in Chapter 5 of the guide.

Remarks

When introducing this activity, the trainer may illustrate the concept of "chapters" by describing those of his or her own life.

FEEDBACK: PRINCIPLES AND PRACTICE

Goals

I. To present criteria for effective feedback.

II. To offer the participants an opportunity to practice giving and receiving feedback.

III. To allow the participants to practice process observation.

Group Size

Flexible.

Time Required

One hour.

Physical Setting

A room large enough to allow a small group to meet within the view of the rest of the participants. Movable chairs should be provided.

Procedure

I. *(Five minutes.)* The trainer introduces the activity, its goals, and the feedback criteria described in The Contexts in Which We Live in Chapter 3 of the guide.

II. *(Twenty minutes.)* The trainer offers to receive feedback related to his or her behavior and asks for three volunteers to give such feedback on the basis of their contact with the trainer thus far. After the volunteers have been obtained, the trainer sits in a part of the room that is visible to all participants and asks the volunteers to sit in a circle around him or her. The remaining participants are instructed to observe the feedback process.

III. *(Ten minutes.)* The trainer and volunteers discuss the feedback given in step II as the rest of the group continues to observe.

IV. *(Fifteen minutes.)* The volunteers rejoin their fellow participants for a total-group discussion of observations. Feedback is offered to the volunteers regarding the style and usefulness of the feedback given the trainer.

V. *(Ten minutes.)* The experience is discussed and evaluated.

USING PERSONAL POWER: A FANTASY EXPERIENCE

Goals

I. To allow the participants to examine their own use of power.

II. To help the participants analyze the facets of their lives in which they do and do not feel powerful.

III. To increase the participants' awareness of the uses of power in their own life situations and relationships.

Group Size

Flexible.

Time Required

One hour.

Physical Setting

A room with flexible seating to allow the participants to be comfortable during a fantasy experience and to work in dyads.

Materials

I. A set of stimulus statements constituting a fantasy experience that requires each participant to envision and reflect on a situation in which he or she feels powerful. These statements, which are prepared by the trainer prior to conducting the activity, can include introductory comments such as the following:

1. Think about a time when you felt in control of yourself and your life.

2. Think about times when you have felt influential with other people.

3. Think about a time when you stood up for something you believe in.

The statements that follow should require the participants to consider power in terms of things they wish they could do.

II. A chalkboard and chalk or a newsprint flip chart and a felt-tipped marker (optional).

Procedure

I. *(Five minutes.)* The activity and its goals are introduced.

II. *(Ten minutes.)* The trainer leads the participants through a short fantasy experience involving personal power. The participants are then asked to form dyads and to share their fantasies with their partners, examining different behaviors, feelings, or changes in perception.

III. *(Five minutes.)* Each participant is asked to continue sharing with a partner by providing five completions for each of the following sentences:

1. I feel powerful when . . . .
2. I feel powerless when . . . .

IV. *(Five minutes.)* The participants are instructed to face their partners, each providing three completions for the following sentence:

If I had power right now, I would . . . .

The trainer then asks the pairs to explore the ways in which they use their personal power as well as the specific situations in which they refrain from using power and why they do so.

V. *(Fifteen minutes.)* The trainer reassembles the total group and leads a discussion in which each participant is asked to focus on answers to the following questions:

1. Am I failing to take advantage of opportunities to use my personal power?
2. What fears do I have about using or abusing my power?
3. How and in what types of situations do I use my power?

The participants' ideas may be recorded on a chalkboard or newsprint if the trainer wishes.

VI. *(Ten minutes.)* The trainer presents illustrations of the uses of power and assertive behavior in personal, job, and group relationships. Comments are included about the nonverbal ways in which power and powerlessness are conveyed. Other points discussed are derived from A Look at Power in Chapter 1 of the guide and from Personal Power in Chapter 3 of the guide.

VII. *(Ten minutes.)* The activity is discussed and evaluated.

IDENTIFYING PERSONAL SUPPORT GROUPS

Goals

I. To allow the participants to examine their present support groups.

II. To explore the benefits of being part of a support group.

III. To help the participants identify ways to strengthen their support groups.

Group Size

Flexible.

Time Required

One hour.

Physical Setting

A room with movable chairs and enough space for the participants to form dyads as well as subgroups of four each.

Materials

A chalkboard and chalk or a newsprint flip chart and a felt-tipped marker.

Procedure

I. *(Ten minutes.)* Using material from Chapter 4 of the guide, the trainer introduces the idea of support groups and explains the importance of such groups to process politicians in particular. The participants' thoughts are elicited regarding the benefits that can be obtained from one's own support group as well as the responsibilities involved in being a member of another person's support group. As these thoughts are contributed, the trainer writes them on a chalkboard or newsprint.

II. *(Ten minutes.)* The participants choose partners based on their impressions of one another as potential members of their support groups and then discuss why they chose each other.

III. *(Fifteen minutes.)* Each pair of participants chooses another pair and discusses the items previously listed by the trainer in relation to their own experiences with support groups.

IV. *(Ten minutes.)* The total group is reassembled, and the trainer leads a discussion of the learnings derived from steps II and III.

V. *(Ten minutes.)* The trainer discusses the rules for relationships listed in Chapter 4 of the guide and expands on the learnings identified by the participants.

VI. *(Five minutes.)* The activity is discussed and evaluated.

Variation

If time permits, the trainer may ask the participants to complete the Support-Group Identification Form (guide, p. 55) as part of step I.

ROLE MODELS:
TEACHING AND LEARNING RELATIONSHIPS

Goals

I. To increase the participants' awareness of their personal teaching and learning networks.

II. To demonstrate that everyone has many teachers and students.

III. To help the participants develop strategies for expanding their learning networks.

Group Size

Flexible.

Time Required

Thirty-five minutes.

Physical Setting

A comfortable room with a writing surface for each participant.

Materials

I. Support-Group Relationship Analysis (guide, p. 56).

II. A pencil or pen for each participant.

III. Blank paper for each participant.

Procedure

I. *(Five minutes.)* The trainer explains that one of the functions of support groups is to provide opportunities to both teach and learn.

II. *(Fifteen minutes.)* Each participant is given a pencil or pen and is asked to complete the Support-Group Relationship Analysis (guide, p. 56).

III. *(Fifteen minutes.)* After distributing blank paper, the trainer requests that each participant make a list of learning goals and decide on action to be taken within the next month toward accomplishing each goal.

Variation

This activity may be expanded by using the steps for developing action plans provided in Chapter 6 of the guide.

TAKING CARE OF ONESELF: REMEDIES FOR BURNOUT

Goals

I. To help the participants assess the ways in which they spend their time.

II. To help the participants determine how they would rather spend their time.

III. To suggest burnout remedies that can be employed immediately.

Group Size

Flexible.

Time Required

One and one-half hours.

Physical Setting

A room large enough to accommodate dyads and to afford comfort during the fantasy experience. Writing surfaces and movable chairs should be provided.

Materials

I. Blank paper for each participant.

II. A pencil or pen for each participant.

III. A copy of the List of Burnout Symptoms, Remedies, and Preventions for each participant.

IV. A set of stimulus statements constituting a fantasy experience in which each participant envisions altering his or her present schedule so that the next month is spent in activities considered ideal. (These statements are prepared by the trainer prior to conducting the activity.)

V. A chalkboard and chalk or a newsprint flip chart and a felt-tipped marker.

Procedure

I. *(Five minutes.)* The activity and its goals are introduced.

II. *(Fifteen minutes.)* After instructing the participants to form dyads, the trainer distributes blank paper and pencils or pens. The partners are asked to take turns interviewing each other and making notes about their activities. Specific questions to be included in the interviews are listed on a chalkboard or newsprint as follows:

   1. Which of your *current activities* give you energy? Which deplete your energy?
   2. Which pertain to your community? your job? your social life? your personal life?
   3. How does the amount of time you spend on each activity compare with the amount of satisfaction it provides you?
   4. In what activities not previously mentioned do you like to participate?
   5. What patterns do you see emerging?

III. *(Ten minutes.)* The total group is reassembled for a discussion of the learnings derived from step II.

IV. *(Twenty minutes.)* The trainer leads the participants through a short fantasy experience involving the creation of an ideal activity schedule. After the conclusion of the experience, the participants are asked to reassemble into dyads, to share their fantasies, and to discuss how they feel about the schedules they envisioned.

V. *(Ten minutes.)* The trainer reconvenes the total group; distributes copies of the List of Burnout Symptoms, Remedies, and Preventions; and discusses the contents of the handout.

VI. *(Fifteen minutes.)* The participants are again asked to select partners and are then instructed to discuss plans for adjusting their activity schedules for the next month so that these schedules more closely resemble those of their fantasies.

VII. *(Ten minutes.)* The total group is again assembled for a discussion of the schedule-adjustment plans developed in step VI. The trainer emphasizes the importance of relying on a support group to help prevent or remedy burnout and encourages the participants to read Chapter 4 of the guide for further information on the subject.

VIII. *(Five minutes.)* The entire activity is discussed and evaluated.

Variation

The trainer may omit the emphasis on individual burnout and focus solely on burnout as it relates to group and organizational activities. In this case the interview questions and the handout should be altered, and the participants should be asked to complete the Activity/Payoff Analysis (guide, p. 48).

List of Burnout Symptoms, Remedies, and Preventions

Individual Burnout

Symptoms

- Tendency to blame others
- Excessive complaints
- Low energy
- Boredom
- Physical illness
- Failure to see friends
- Misplaced priorities
- Feeling of being overwhelmed
- Agitation
- Denial of burnout
- Insomnia
- Feeling of being trapped
- Fatigue
- Short temper
- Chemical abuse
- Decreased creativity
- Nonproductivity while busy
- Inability to focus on matters at hand
- Dejection
- Absence of physical well being
- Feeling of ineffectiveness
- Lack of enthusiasm

Remedies

1. Ask for help.
2. Examine priorities.
3. Choose to become burned out for a set period of time.
4. Contact support-group members for help.
5. Take a week off.
6. Engage in energizing activities.
7. Examine the balance between personal time, social time, family time, and work time.
8. Go on an enjoyable retreat.
9. Take a leave of absence.
10. Ask for feedback about personal use of chemicals.
11. Inform others of the feeling of burnout and of personal plans to take a "sabbatical."
12. Take a "mental-health" break.
13. Meditate.
14. Obtain more sleep.

Group and Organizational Burnout

Symptoms

- Nonproductive, nervous energy while working on tasks
- Little energy for accomplishing maintenance concerns
- Tendency to blame "outside" forces
- Nonproductive meetings
- Requests for relief
- Members or co-workers exhibit each other's negative symptoms.

Remedies

1. Ask for help from fellow group members or co-workers.
2. Ask for help from an outsider.
3. Go on an enjoyable retreat.
4. Suspend operations until the group feels capable of resuming.
5. Eliminate such activities as meetings that last until late at night as well as those that are held during mealtime.
6. Recognize that everyone will lose unless an effort is made to recover.
7. Recognize that the situation is systemic and requires a major intervention.

Preventive Measures

1. Plan regular retreats for fun and a change of perspective.
2. Make a list every day of priority activities to be completed as well as activities that can be delayed.
3. Schedule weekly "maintenance" meetings with fellow group members or co-workers.
4. Develop an awareness of the circumstances that generate burn-out.
5. Say "no."
6. Avoid stressful situations or groups.
7. With the help of support-group members, examine options in various situations.
8. Meditate.
9. Include considerations of benefits, success, and visible results as part of planning processes.
10. Take a leave of absence or vacation when symptoms of burnout begin to appear.

11. Renegotiate roles.
12. Keep priorities in order.
13. Be aware of and take advantage of personal energy cycles.
14. Identify and make use of a personal support base.

BASIC GROUP DYNAMICS: AN INTERACTION

Goals

  I. To enable the participants to experience the dynamics involved in group decision making.
 II. To provide the participants with practice in process observation and feedback.
III. To help the participants gain an understanding of basic group dynamics.

Group Size

A minimum of twelve participants.

Time Required

One hour and twenty-five minutes.

Physical Setting

A room large enough to accommodate subgroups of approximately six participants each. Writing surfaces and movable chairs should be provided.

Materials

  I. A chalkboard and chalk or a newsprint flip chart and a felt-tipped marker.
 II. Figure 1, Sample Process-Observation Report Form (guide, p. 71).
III. A pencil or pen for each participant.
 IV. A copy of the Group-Process Analysis for each participant plus an additional copy for each subgroup.
  V. A copy of the Group-Development Handout for each participant.

Procedure

  I. *(Five minutes.)* The activity and its goals are introduced.

II. *(Ten minutes.)* The trainer elicits the participants' responses regarding the various groups to which they have belonged; records these responses on a chalkboard or newsprint; and, with the help of the participants, arranges the responses according to group type (community or work groups, boards of directors, advisory committees, and so forth).

III. *(Ten minutes.)* Each participant is given a pencil or pen and a copy of the Group-Process Analysis and is asked to complete the analysis.

IV. *(Twenty minutes.)* The participants divide into subgroups of approximately six each, and each subgroup selects one of its members to serve as *recorder* and another to serve as *process observer.* The trainer then gives each subgroup a blank copy of the Group-Process Analysis and asks the members of each subgroup to arrive at a consensus response to each statement on the analysis. Each subgroup's recorder completes the analysis in accordance with the consensus decision about each statement, and the process observer observes the interactions of the members and completes the Sample Process-Observation Report Form (Figure 1 in the guide, p. 71).

V. *(Ten minutes.)* The trainer stops the work of the subgroups after fifteen minutes, regardless of their progress in completing the task, and asks the members of each subgroup to spend a few minutes discussing their feelings about their progress. The process observers are asked to give feedback regarding the behaviors they noted.

VI. *(Ten minutes.)* The total group is reassembled, and each participant receives a copy of the Group-Development Handout. The trainer discusses the handout by explaining such principles of group dynamics as developmental phases, members' roles and functions, and leadership.

VII. *(Fifteen minutes.)* Focusing on the points made by the trainer in step VI, the participants share their own experiences of group dynamics as they completed the subgroup work.

VIII. *(Five minutes.)* The activity is discussed and evaluated.

Group-Process Analysis

Indicate whether you agree or disagree with each of the following statements by marking an X in the appropriate blank.

Agree   Disagree

_____   _____ 1. A primary concern of all group members should be to establish an atmosphere in which everyone feels free to express personal opinions.

_____   _____ 2. Individual members are able to achieve greater personal security in a group with a strong leader than in a leaderless group.

_____   _____ 3. Often there are times when an individual who is part of a working group should do what he or she thinks is right, regardless of what the group has decided to do.

_____   _____ 4. Members should be required to attend meetings at which group goals are to be set and group problems are to be discussed.

_____   _____ 5. Generally, there comes a time when democratic methods must be abandoned in order to solve practical problems.

_____   _____ 6. In the long run, it is more important to use democratic methods than to achieve specific results by other means.

_____   _____ 7. Sometimes it is necessary for a person to require fellow group members to change as he or she thinks is right, even when they object.

_____   _____ 8. It is sometimes necessary to ignore the feelings of others in order to reach a group decision.

_____   _____ 9. When the leader is doing his or her best, the other members should not openly criticize or find fault with his or her conduct.

_____   _____ 10. Attentiveness in meetings can be increased by adopting a policy whereby the leader comes to the point and says what he or she wants the group to do.

Agree   Disagree

_____   _____   11. Democracy has no place in a military organization, an air task force, or an infantry squad when actually in battle.

_____   _____   12. By the time the average person has reached maturity, it is almost impossible for him or her to increase personal skill in group participation.

_____   _____   13. When every member of a group must be considered before decisions are made, attendance at meetings drops.

_____   _____   14. Group membership does not dwindle when the chairperson is careful to choose friends as members.

Group-Development Handout

Developmental Phase	Characteristics	Appropriate Action to Be Taken
Dependence	1. Few members participate.	1. Actively include members in discussions at a low-risk level.
	2. The leader is allowed to be in charge.	2. Support the skills that the members already possess.
	3. The leader must push for implementation of decisions.	3. Pay attention to maintenance activities.
	4. Members appear passive.	
Counterdependence	1. The leader is frequently challenged by the members.	1. Acknowledge what is happening in the group.
	2. A great deal of behind-the-scenes activity takes place.	2. Encourage the leader to seek support from his or her friends.
	3. The leader feels puzzled and ineffective.	3. Actively include members in discussions and activities.
	4. The leader and the members feel separate from each other.	4. Seek a variety of viewpoints on each issue; encourage members to voice differences of opinion.
	5. Decisions are not carried out.	5. Rotate the responsibility for facilitation.
	6. The members blame the leader for the group's problems.	6. Clarify issues.
	7. Cliques are formed.	7. Encourage members to accept responsibility and to follow through.
	8. Internal personality clashes are evident.	
Interdependence	1. A balance exists between task and maintenance activities.	1. Maintain a regular process for integrating new members.
	2. Humor is manifested.	2. Focus consciously on both task and maintenance concerns.
	3. Friendships develop outside meetings.	3. Incorporate time to celebrate successes.
	4. Roles are comfortable and understood.	4. Have a yearly retreat or social gathering to cement relations and to plan for the future.

LEADERSHIP STYLES: A PERSONAL ASSESSMENT

Goals

I. To enable the participants to examine their own concepts and styles of leadership.

II. To examine the qualities that differentiate a leader from a follower.

III. To identify ways in which the participants can transfer learnings to group situations outside the session.

Group Size

A maximum of thirty participants.

Time Required

Two hours and fifteen minutes.

Physical Setting

A room with a work table and movable chairs for each subgroup of approximately five participants.

Materials

I. A set of art supplies for each subgroup. Each set should be assembled by the trainer prior to conducting the activity and should include materials such as the following: blank paper, construction paper, felt-tipped markers in various colors, tape, scissors, straws, and pipe cleaners.

II. A chalkboard and chalk or a newsprint flip chart and a felt-tipped marker.

III. A copy of the Model of Leadership Styles for each participant.

Procedure

I. *(Five minutes.)* The trainer introduces the activity and its goals, presenting the definition of leadership provided in Chapter 5 of the guide.

II. *(Forty-five minutes.)* The participants are asked to form subgroups of approximately five each, and each subgroup is asked to be seated at a work table. The trainer distributes sets of art supplies and asks each subgroup to construct a visual representation of that subgroup's concept of leadership.

III. *(Twenty minutes.)* After approximately forty minutes, the trainer stops the progress of the artwork and asks the participants to remain in their subgroups and to discuss their experiences during the previous step. Specific questions to be considered in these discussions are listed on a chalkboard or newsprint as follows:

1. How were decisions made?
2. Who emerged as leader(s)?
3. Was leadership shared?
4. How did it feel to be leaders or followers?
5. What did you learn about yourselves?
6. What type of balance was established between task and maintenance activities?
7. Which members assumed which roles?

IV. *(Fifteen minutes.)* The total group is reconvened, and the trainer leads a discussion on the concepts of leadership generated in the subgroups.

V. *(Fifteen minutes.)* The trainer distributes copies of the Model of Leadership Styles to all participants, discusses the contents of this handout, and relates the model to the concepts generated in the subgroups. It is recommended that the participants read the following material from Chapter 5 of the guide: Roles of Group Members, Leadership, Decision Making, Conflict, and Motivation.

VI. *(Fifteen minutes.)* The participants are asked to assemble into subgroups of two or three each and to discuss the learnings derived from the activity, ways in which these learnings can be applied to situations outside the workshop environment, and ways in which they can increase their effectiveness as leaders.

VII. *(Twenty minutes.)* The total group is again reconvened, and the entire activity is discussed and evaluated.

Model of Leadership Styles

Type of Leadership	Advantages	Disadvantages
Task-Oriented Leader	1. The group reaps the benefits of the leader's competence and urge to excel. 2. Because of the leader's strong sense of task, much is accomplished. 3. The leader experiences a great deal of satisfaction.	1. The group experiences disintegration. 2. The leader pays too much attention to intellectual analysis of issues. 3. The members are subject to the leader's discrimination. 4. The leader sacrifices group cohesiveness to his or her own sense of satisfaction and productivity.
Process (Shared) Leadership	1. All members experience ownership. 2. Because all members are part of the process, they are committed to group goals. 3. Group cohesiveness is maximized. 4. Sharing of ego satisfaction exists within the group. 5. Democratic living is experienced. 6. Individual growth occurs as a result of assuming responsibility, exercising skills, and so forth.	1. No one (or everyone) assumes ultimate responsibility for the completion of specific tasks. 2. Confusion exists regarding the identity of the "leader."
Maintenance-Oriented Leader	1. The members receive good "parenting." 2. Fellowship is experienced. 3. The members feel supported personally.	1. Too much support is provided by the leader. 2. The group fails to concentrate on tasks and therefore accomplishes little. 3. The leader denies or fails to take advantage of his or her own expertise.

ACTION PLANNING AND EVALUATION

Goals

I. To present the principles of action planning.

II. To give the participants an opportunity to experience action-planning processes.

Group Size

A maximum of thirty participants.

Time Required

Two hours and twenty minutes.

Physical Setting

A large room with flexible seating to accommodate subgroups of four to six participants each.

Materials

A chalkboard and chalk or a newsprint flip chart and a felt-tipped marker.

Procedure

I. *(Twenty minutes.)* The trainer introduces the activity, briefly reviews its goals, and then facilitates the development of either a real or fictitious case study involving an issue of the group's choosing. Highlights of the study are written on a chalkboard or newsprint for the participants' reference.

II. *(Thirty minutes.)* Using the questions presented in Steps for Developing Action Plans, step 3, in Chapter 6 of the guide, the trainer leads the group in composing a problem statement.

III. *(Fifteen minutes.)* The trainer covers the remaining steps and skills required for action planning (derived from Steps for Developing Action Plans in Chapter 6 of the guide).

IV. *(Forty-five minutes.)* The participants are asked to form sub-groups of four to six each. Each subgroup chooses one of its members to function as a facilitator as the subgroup completes the steps of the action-planning process and arrives at an approach to solving the problem presented in the case study.

V. *(Fifteen minutes.)* After approximately forty minutes, the trainer stops the action-planning process and instructs the subgroups to discuss the interactions experienced during this process. If desired, each subgroup may choose a new member facilitator to fulfill this function during the discussion. Specific areas of focus for the subgroup discussions are listed on a chalkboard or newsprint as follows:

1. The subgroup's energy level and satisfaction with the experience;
2. Ways in which the experience could be improved; and
3. What the subgroup might want to do next to solve the case-study problem.

VI. *(Fifteen minutes.)* The trainer reconvenes the total group and leads a concluding discussion, highlighting the principles of action planning and evaluation that arose during the course of the activity.

POSITIVE THINKING: PLANNING FOR SUCCESS

Goals

I. To allow the participants to experience a planning process that focuses on possibilities rather than problems related to accomplishing a goal.

II. To provide the participants with insight into the ways in which this planning process can be used by groups.

Group Size

Flexible.

Time Required

One hour and fifteen minutes.

Physical Setting

A large, carpeted room in which the participants can be comfortable during a fantasy experience. Writing surfaces should be provided, and seating should be flexible to accommodate work in dyads.

Materials

I. A copy of the Positive-Planning Work Sheet for each participant.

II. A pencil or pen for each participant.

III. A set of stimulus statements constituting a fantasy experience in which each participant is asked to think about an area of personal concern and to visualize that situation as it would be if it were perfect. (These statements are prepared by the trainer prior to conducting the activity. They should evoke specific images of the people involved in the situation, the setting, the action in which the participant is engaged, and the participant's feelings about the situation.)

Procedure

I. *(Five minutes.)* The trainer introduces the activity and its goals, providing an overview of the concept of positive planning.

II. *(Fifteen minutes.)* Each participant is asked to become as comfortable and relaxed as possible. The trainer leads the participants through a fantasy experience in which a situation of personal concern is visualized as perfect.

III. *(Fifteen minutes.)* The trainer distributes copies of the Positive-Planning Work Sheet and pencils or pens and asks the participants to complete the first two items on the work sheet.

IV. *(Twenty minutes.)* Each participant is instructed to select a partner with whom he or she feels comfortable and to complete items 3 and 4 on the work sheet.

V. *(Twenty minutes.)* The trainer reassembles the total group and invites the participants to share their thoughts and feelings about the experience as well as the possible applications of positive planning in group environments.

Variation

This activity may be used with an ongoing work group that is trying to achieve a particular goal, or it may be employed as the initial phase in a long-range planning process for an organization or group.

Remarks

The success of this activity is largely dependent on the trainer's ability to generate enthusiasm and an atmosphere of positive thinking and support among the participants. During step IV in particular, the trainer should encourage the participants to view the specifics of their fantasy situations as positive successes.

Positive-Planning Work Sheet

The traditional model of planning focuses on what is *wrong* in a given situation; positive planning, in contrast, is the art of concentrating on and celebrating what is *right.* You have just completed the first step of positive planning by visualizing a situation of personal concern as it would be if it were perfect. By completing this work sheet, you can further the process of planning in a positive way to achieve your goals in this situation.

1. Describe your perfect image in detail by answering the following questions:

   Who is involved?

   What is the setting?

   What are you doing?

   What are other people doing?

   How do you feel as you visualize your ideal situation?

Developed by Betty Aldridge and Warren Sam Miller.

2. List as many other specifics about your ideal image as you can. These specifics can be seen as your long-range goals.

3. Describe your ideal image to your partner. As you go through your list of specifics, check the items that describe your actual situation.

4. Mark with an asterisk (*) the items on your list that need attention and action. List those items in the appropriate column below. Next list the specific, short-term action steps you plan to take in connection with each item and establish a reasonable completion date for each action step.

Item   **Action**   **Completion Date**

EFFECTIVE COMMUNICATION: LEARNING BASIC SKILLS

Goals

I. To increase the participants' awareness of their interpersonal communication patterns.

II. To identify the skills necessary for effective communication.

III. To help the participants identify individual change goals with regard to their communication patterns.

Group Size

Flexible.

Time Required

One hour and fifteen minutes.

Physical Setting

A room with flexible seating and adequate space to accommodate triads.

Procedure

I. *(Five minutes.)* The trainer introduces the activity and its goals.

II. *(Fifteen minutes.)* The participants are asked to form triads, and each triad member is asked to assume one of the following roles:

1. A speaker who describes what he or she believes to be the features of positive communication;

2. A respondent who repeats what was said about communication; and

3. An observer who witnesses the verbal and nonverbal interactions between the speaker and the respondent.

The interchange is completed as described above. Then the members of each triad switch roles, repeat the interchange, switch again, and repeat the interchange again so that each participant has a chance to serve in each role.

III. *(Ten minutes.)* The triad members discuss the experience of the previous step, including their observations of each other's body language, posture, voice tone, eye contact, and so forth.

IV. *(Fifteen minutes.)* The trainer reassembles the total group, refers the participants to the communication diagram in Chapter 7 of the guide (p. 100), and reviews the basic skills involved in effective communication.

V. *(Ten minutes.)* The participants discuss comparisons between their triad conversations and the diagram framework.

VI. *(Ten minutes.)* The trainer invites each participant to identify some aspect of his or her own communication style that could be improved and to share intentions for improvement with the total group.

VII. *(Ten minutes.)* The activity is discussed and evaluated.

Variations

I. If this activity is used with an ongoing group, the speakers in each triad may be asked to talk about positive communication patterns that they have observed within that group.

II. Step IV may be expanded to include a discussion of the negative communication styles (blamer, placater, computer, and distracter) described in Basic Communication Skills in Chapter 7 of the guide.

SUCCESSFUL MEETINGS: CLARIFYING AND EVALUATING

Goals

I. To build a definition of a "successful" meeting.

II To identify techniques and guidelines that foster success in meetings.

III. To identify typical problems that arise during meetings and some ways of minimizing those problems.

IV. To demonstrate one technique for evaluating a meeting.

Group Size

A maximum of fifty participants.

Time Required

One hour and twenty-five minutes.

Physical Setting

A room with flexible seating and sufficient space to accommodate subgroups of approximately five participants each.

Materials

I. A chalkboard and chalk or a newsprint flip chart and a felt-tipped marker.

II. Blank paper for each subgroup recorder.

III. A pencil or pen for each subgroup recorder.

IV. A clipboard or other portable writing surface for each subgroup recorder.

Procedure

I. *(Five minutes.)* The trainer introduces the activity and its goals. It is emphasized that although certain techniques can be used to make meetings effective, no standard rules exist regarding the ways in which meetings must be conducted.

II. *(Ten minutes.)* The total group brainstorms indicators of success in meetings. The trainer lists these indicators on a chalkboard or newsprint and stresses behavioral cues as well as personal feelings that the participants have experienced.

III. *(Twenty minutes.)* The participants assemble into subgroups of approximately five each, and each subgroup selects a recorder. The trainer gives blank paper, a pencil or pen, and a clipboard or other portable writing surface to each recorder along with instructions to make notes as the subgroup members discuss methods for facilitating meetings and making them successful.

IV. *(Fifteen minutes.)* The total group is reconvened. As the recorders share their subgroups' ideas, the trainer writes these ideas on a chalkboard or newsprint and supplements them with material derived from Chapter 7 of the guide.

V. *(Twenty minutes.)* Comments are elicited regarding problems that the participants have encountered during meetings. A total-group consultation is conducted with the objective of determining ways to handle such problems.

VI. *(Ten minutes.)* The trainer summarizes the participants' contributions of techniques for fostering success in meetings and for coping with problems that arise.

VII. *(Five minutes.)* To evaluate the activity and to practice one technique for evaluating a meeting, the participants describe what they liked or disliked about the experience and what they learned.

BEHIND THE SCENES:
EXAMINING INFORMAL GROUP ACTIVITIES

Goals

I. To increase the participants' awareness of the types of group activities that occur behind the scenes.

II. To identify some helpful as well as harmful results of behind-the-scenes activities.

Group Size

Flexible.

Time Required

Thirty minutes.

Physical Setting

A room with writing surfaces for the participants.

Materials

I. Blank paper for each participant.

II. A pencil or pen for each participant.

III. A chalkboard and chalk or a newsprint flip chart and a felt-tipped marker.

Procedure

I. *(Five minutes.)* The trainer introduces the activity, referring to Chapter 8 of the guide.

II. *(Fifteen minutes.)* After distributing blank paper and pencils or pens, the trainer asks each participant to think about a group of which he or she is an active member, to list the names of other group members with whom he or she has had behind-the-scenes contact, and to write a description of each contact by supplying the following information:

1. Who initiated the contact;

68

2. What happened; and

3. What type of impact the incident had on group effectiveness.

III. *(Ten minutes.)* The trainer invites the participants to share information about their behind-the-scenes activities as well as their general observations regarding the importance of such activities. During this discussion the trainer lists on a chalkboard or newsprint the advantages and disadvantages of behind-the-scenes contacts as identified by the participants.

Variation

With an ongoing group, the trainer may ask the members to examine the behind-the-scenes activities in their own group. General discussion focuses on the ways in which these contacts have promoted or hindered group effectiveness.

GROUP CONSULTANTS:
IDENTIFYING VALUABLE NONMEMBERS

Goal

To identify the ways in which nonmembers contribute to a group's effectiveness without attending meetings.

Group Size

Flexible.

Time Required

Thirty minutes.

Physical Setting

A room with writing surfaces for the participants.

Materials

I. Blank paper for each participant.

II. A pencil or pen for each participant.

III. A chalkboard and chalk or a newsprint flip chart and a felt-tipped marker.

Procedure

I. *(Five minutes.)* The trainer introduces the activity, referring to Extragroup Dynamics and Behind-the-Scenes Personalities in Chapter 8 of the guide.

II. *(Ten minutes.)* After distributing blank paper and pencils or pens, the trainer asks each participant to make a list of behind-the-scenes contributors to a group in which he or she is active.

III. *(Fifteen minutes.)* Responses are elicited regarding the types of behind-the-scenes consultants identified by the participants. The trainer lists the participants' responses on a chalkboard or newsprint and leads a general discussion about the value of nonmembers' roles.

Variations

I. With an ongoing group, the trainer may ask the members to establish a list of outside consultants and their contributions so that these people can be formally thanked.

II. If time permits, the participants may be asked to identify their unmet consultant needs and to make plans to meet those needs in accordance with the action-planning steps provided in Chapter 6 of the guide.

CONFLICT RESOLUTION: AN OVERVIEW

Goals

I. To introduce the participants to the four basic responses to conflict.

II. To examine the levels of satisfaction associated with each response.

III. To acquaint the participants with some specific skills for successfully resolving conflict situations.

Group Size

A minimum of nine participants.

Time Required

One hour.

Physical Setting

A comfortable room with writing surfaces for the participants and with flexible seating to accommodate triads.

Materials

I. Blank paper for each participant.

II. A pencil or pen for each participant.

III. A copy of A Brief Primer on Conflict for each participant.

IV. A chalkboard and chalk or a newsprint flip chart and a felt-tipped marker.

Procedure

I. *(Five minutes.)* The activity and its goals are introduced.

II. *(Ten minutes.)* The trainer prepares the participants for a fantasy experience by asking them to become as comfortable and relaxed as possible. Then the trainer reads the following stimulus statements, pausing after each statement to give the participants time to visualize:

You are walking down the street and you see someone several blocks away who is walking toward you. As you continue walking, you eventually recognize the person as someone with whom you are currently in conflict. Thoughts quickly occur to you about alternative actions that you can take; however, before you are able to decide what to do, you find yourself face to face with the person. You have to choose an alternative *now*. You make a choice, act on it, and the interaction is over. You walk on and take some time to examine your feelings and your level of satisfaction with what took place.

The participants are brought out of the fantasy and back to the present.

III. *(Five minutes.)* The trainer distributes blank paper and pencils or pens and instructs each participant to list each alternative considered, to indicate the one that was selected, and to describe the level of satisfaction (high, medium, or low) connected with each alternative.

IV. *(Fifteen minutes.)* The participants are asked to form triads. The members of each triad select a recorder, who makes notes as they discuss their various action alternatives and the levels of satisfaction associated with these alternatives.

V. *(Ten minutes.)* The trainer reconvenes the total group, asks the recorders to report the results of the triad discussions, and lists these results on a chalkboard or newsprint.

VI. *(Ten minutes.)* Copies of A Brief Primer on Conflict are distributed to all participants. Using the content of the triad discussions as well as that of the handout, the trainer points out the four basic resonses to conflict and leads a discussion about the level of satisfaction generally produced by each response. The theory of win/win and the negotiation approach are emphasized, and it is suggested that the participants review the material presented in Basic Communication Skills in Chapter 7 of the guide as well as that provided in Conflict-Resolution Skills in Chapter 9 of the guide.

VII. *(Five minutes.)* The activity is discussed and evaluated.

Variation

This activity may be used with an ongoing group as the first step toward resolution of conflicts between members.

A Brief Primer on Conflict

Conflict is a reality that we all face daily. Whenever our needs or values come into opposition with those of others, conflict invariably results.

Some conflicts are minor and relatively easy to handle. Others are of greater magnitude and require the use of strategies and skills if they are to be resolved successfully. Although we are presented with few formal opportunities to learn these strategies and skills, the effectiveness with which we interact with others is largely determined by our abilities to use these skills.

Sources of Conflict

Conflict can develop as a result of differences in any of the following areas:

- Class
- Values
- Goals
- Philosophy
- Tactics
- Styles

Dimensions of Conflict

The dimensions of conflict to be analyzed are represented by the following questions:

- What is the source of the conflict?
- What are the tangible effects of the conflict?
- Who is interested in resolving the conflict?
- How would the situation appear if the conflict were resolved?

Arenas of Conflict

The arenas in which conflict occurs are as follows:

- Within the individual (*intrapersonal* conflict);
- Between individuals (*interpersonal* conflict);
- Within a group (*intragroup* conflict); and
- Between groups (*intergroup* conflict).

Adapted from *Interpersonal Conflict Management*, an Alternative Behavior Associates Publication by Jack Worel, 1976. Used with permission.

Responses to Conflict

The four basic responses to conflict are as follows:

1. *Fight*, in which one party assumes power over another, confrontation occurs, and a win/lose situation results;
2. *Flight*, in which the conflict issue is avoided rather than resolved and a low level of satisfaction results;
3. *Defusion*, in which the parties involved seek temporary alleviation of the immediate situation and which results in partial resolution, low satisfaction, and confusion regarding the real issues; and
4. *Negotiation*, in which those involved work toward a win/win solution and which results in clarity of issues, a number of options for conflict resolution, and high-level satisfaction for all parties.

Strategies and Skills for Conflict Resolution

The following strategies and skills are useful in negotiating conflict resolution:

1. *Diagnosing*, in which the type and source of the conflict are identified;
2. *Initiating*, in which individual desires to resolve the conflict are stated clearly, effectively, and in a way that ensures receptiveness rather than defensiveness on the part of others;
3. *Listening*, which involves an earnest effort to truly hear what others are saying and a willingness to involve an impartial "third party" to facilitate communication if necessary; and
4. *Problem solving*, in which the issues are clarified, options are identified, a solution is chosen, and implementation as well as evaluation of the solution are planned.

"LAST-DITCH" STRATEGIES: A BRAINSTORMING ACTIVITY[2]

Goals

I. To provide the participants with an opportunity to experience the value of group resources in problem-solving efforts.

II. To demonstrate the creativity that a group can generate.

Group Size

A minimum of five and a maximum of fifteen participants.

Time Required

One hour.

Physical Setting

A room with chairs arranged in such a way that everyone faces the trainer. Writing surfaces should be provided for the participants.

Materials

I. Blank paper for each participant.

II. A pencil or pen for each participant.

III. A chalkboard and chalk or a newsprint flip chart and a felt-tipped marker.

Procedure

I. *(Ten minutes.)* The trainer introduces the activity by explaining the goals and by mentioning the fact that anyone who belongs to a group occasionally experiences a situation in which he or she simply does not know what to do to help that group solve a particular problem. The participants are asked to consider whether they are currently experiencing such situations, and a

---

[2]Adapted from a seminar design developed by Mike Groh, Minneapolis, Minnesota, 1974. Used with permission.

volunteer is asked to share a group problem with which he or she needs help.

II. *(Ten minutes.)* After a specific problem has been presented, the trainer distributes blank paper and pencils or pens and asks each participant to list all solutions that come to mind, regardless of whether these solutions seem practical.

III. *(Fifteen minutes.)* The trainer asks each participant in turn to share one solution idea from his or her list. Each solution is numbered and written on a chalkboard or newsprint, but is not critiqued.

IV. *(Fifteen minutes.)* The process of step III is repeated until the participants' ideas have been exhausted. When an individual participant no longer has written solutions to share, he or she may either pass for that round or contribute an idea generated from the sharing. All solutions, including those that seem ludicrous, are listed.

V. *(Ten minutes.)* The trainer asks each participant to privately compare the total number of ideas generated with the number that he or she personally listed. Since the group total is usually much larger than anyone's individual total, the trainer uses this fact to illustrate the principle that a well-functioning group has access to more ideas for problem solution than its members have separately. It is further pointed out that because all ideas listed on the chalkboard or newsprint represent potential solutions, the process of arriving at a final solution is mainly a question of selecting and combining the members' ideas. In conclusion, the trainer recommends that the participants read the material presented in Identifying the Situation in Chapter 10 of the guide.

Variations

I. With a larger group, the trainer may ask the participants to form subgroups in which the brainstorming process is completed.

II. If time permits, the trainer may help the participants choose a solution from the list of alternatives and then develop a plan of action.

III. To allow each participant to obtain help with a group problem, the trainer may divide the total group into triads consisting of individuals who do not usually work together. Each triad member then explains his or her problem and seeks possible solutions from the other two triad members. The trainer encourages the participants to enjoy themselves and to place a premium on seemingly unlikely solutions in order to foster creative thinking.

BUILDING A SYSTEM MOBILE

Goals

I. To illustrate differences and similarities in the ways in which individuals perceive organizational systems.

II. To examine the power relationships that exist among a system's components.

Group Size

A minimum of eight participants.

Time Required

One hour and five minutes.

Physical Setting

A room with a work table and movable chairs for each subgroup of four to six participants.

Materials

A set of art supplies and building materials for each subgroup. Each set should be assembled by the trainer prior to conducting the activity and should include materials such as the following: colored construction paper, pencils, crayons, felt-tipped markers in various colors, tape, glue, string, scissors, Tinker Toys,® straws, pipe cleaners, and paper clips.

Procedure

I. *(Five minutes.)* The trainer introduces the activity and its goals and presents the definition of the term "system" provided in Systems and Their Values in Chapter 11 of the guide. The participants are directed to form subgroups of four to six each, and each subgroup is asked to be seated at a work table.

II. *(Twenty minutes.)* The trainer assigns each subgroup a different system to analyze; system alternatives include organizations such as a *church,* a *business,* a *professional association,* and a *neighborhood.* Each subgroup is then given a set of art supplies and building materials and is instructed to build a mobile illustrating the structure of the assigned system as the members perceive it. It is further emphasized that each mobile should portray the power relationships that exist among the components of the system.

III. *(Ten minutes.)* After the mobiles have been completed, each subgroup is asked to assess the way in which each member's ideas were incorporated into the mobile. The trainer points out that during this discussion the members should examine the manifestations of influence, leadership, and decision making in their subgroup.

IV. *(Fifteen minutes.)* The total group is reassembled, and the trainer instructs the members of each subgroup to present and explain their mobile and to share their experiences during the building process.

V. *(Ten minutes.)* The trainer summarizes the principles of power and leadership as evidenced in the participants' comments in step IV. In addition, the content of Power in Chapter 2 of the guide and of Leadership in Chapter 5 of the guide is discussed. Particular emphasis is placed on the issue of the balance of power among groups within a system.

VI. *(Five minutes.)* The activity is discussed and evaluated.

Remarks

If this design is used with an ongoing group, the trainer should be aware that conflicts may erupt as a result of the fact that the group members know each other well.

INSTITUTIONAL VALUES: A ROLE-PLAY ACTIVITY

Goals

I. To allow the participants to experience the effects of conflicting motivations.

II. To increase the participants' awareness of the self-interest issues and values underlying the role-play interactions.

III. To provide the participants with an opportunity to practice process observation.

IV. To help the participants recognize the effects of institutional values on group decision making.

Group Size

From sixteen to twenty participants.

Time Required

Two hours.

Physical Setting

A large room with tables and chairs arranged so that the role players can see each other and the process observers are seated on the periphery.

Materials

I. A copy of the Role-Play Instructions for each participant.

II. Blank paper for each process observer.

III. A pencil or pen for each process observer.

Procedure

I. *(Ten minutes.)* The trainer introduces the activity and its goals and presents the role-play situation as an opportunity to experience some of the dynamics at work in an institutional or system setting. It is stressed that the learning emphasis in this activity is on the *process* rather than the end product of the simulation.

II. *(Fifteen minutes.)* Preparation for the simulation is accomplished as follows:

1. The trainer gives everyone a copy of the Role-Play Instructions and asks the participants to read this handout carefully.

2. One participant is selected for each of the eight roles, and the remaining participants are informed that they are to be process observers.

3. Each role player is instructed to study his or her role description and to prepare to act in the interest of the organization that he or she represents.

4. While the role players are preparing for the simulation, the trainer distributes blank paper and pencils or pens to all process observers and then clarifies their task, explaining that as they observe the simulation they are to identify the power source among the role players and to make notes regarding the specific behavioral data that support their conclusions.

III. *(Thirty minutes.)* The simulation takes place.

IV. *(Thirty minutes.)* To debrief the role players, the trainer asks them to share individually their experiences during the simulation and to discuss any unresolved feelings they have as a result of their experiences. Then, as the observers share their observations and conclusions, the trainer facilitates this process in order to focus on the issue of power as it relates to motivation and values. Questions such as the following are asked:

1. What did each person have to gain or lose in the situation?

2. What alliances were formed?

3. How did people's roles affect their perceptions of "right" and "wrong"?

4. What conflicts arose? How were they dealt with?

V. *(Twenty-five minutes.)* Using material from Chapter 11 of the guide as well as the simulation experience, the trainer discusses the principles of personal and institutional values, the interplay of these two sets of values, ways to recognize situations in which institutional values are an issue, and ways to deal with such situations.

VI. *(Ten minutes.)* The activity and the participants' personal learnings are discussed and evaluated.

Variations

I. The trainer may choose not to provide all participants with all role descriptions; instead, he or she may simply describe the situation involved in the simulation and then give each role description only to the appropriate role player.

II. With a larger group, the trainer may develop and assign additional roles or ask more than one participant to assume each role.

III. If desired, the role-play situation may be altered to reflect the participants' specific group experiences.

Role-Play Instructions

Situation

The hospital administrator has called a meeting of the representatives of various groups and interests in the community and within the structure of the local hospital. The purpose of the meeting is to discuss the hospital's application for a permit to purchase a cancer-treatment machine at a cost of $977,000. The administrator would like to obtain the representatives' support for this application.

Hospital Administrator

1. You want to have a positive impact on the hospital's system of health-care delivery.
2. You like your $55,000-a-year job.
3. You have been instructed by the hospital's board of directors to cut health-care costs.
4. You are under pressure from the medical staff to advocate the purchase of the cancer-treatment machine.
5. The hospital is subject to a growing number of government regulations requiring permits to acquire new equipment or to expand physical facilities. Completing the paperwork associated with obtaining each permit is a time-consuming task for which you are responsible.

Insurance-Company Representative

1. You are committed to providing good health-care coverage for your subscribers so that individuals do not have to spend their own money to pay for medical services.
2. You want to see your company profits increase next year in accordance with the company goals that were set and announced last week.
3. You are beginning to feel pressure from some policyholders to provide coverage for nontraditional treatment approaches, such as acupuncture and at-home births.

Community Resident

1. You represent a neighborhood group that wants more preventive health-care programs emphasizing prevention, but instead you see such programs being decreased due to insurance-company regulations against covering this type of service.
2. Your group opposes the parking ramp that the hospital is planning to construct in a residential neighborhood.
3. You are unable to afford health insurance, but earn too much money to qualify for public medical assistance.

Nursing Supervisor

1. You were just told that you cannot fill the two vacant positions on your staff because of financial "belt tightening" within the hospital.
2. You entered the profession of nursing because you care about people.

Government Monitor

1. Your job is to enforce the administration's policy of lowering health-care costs.
2. Your department within the government is subject to intense lobbying pressures for the medical profession to maintain high standards of health-care service.
3. You are aware that the two other cancer-treatment machines in the city are currently underutilized.

Chief of Hospital Medical Staff

1. You have had a long and productive career with the hospital.
2. You want the hospital to purchase the cancer-treatment machine as part of a program to become a cancer-treatment center within the city.
3. One of your incentives for working at this hospital is its good physician benefits (private and free parking, free coffee, regular banquets, access to funds for in-service training, and so forth).

Patient Advocate

1. You were hired two years ago as a result of community pressure.
2. You were just informed that your position will be eliminated in three months because the insurance company will not reimburse the hospital for the cost of your salary.

Consumer of Services

1. You live in the neighborhood adjacent to the hospital.
2. You are interested in joining a health-maintenance organization that operates on a prepaid basis, but your community currently has no such organization.

MAGIC WAND: PERSONAL ACTION PLANNING

Goals

I. To help the participants relate their workshop learnings to their current life situations.

II. To assist each participant in identifying a specific goal to pursue regarding a selected group and in developing a strategy for action directed toward achieving that goal.

Group Size

Flexible.

Time Required

One hour.

Physical Setting

A room with movable chairs, writing surfaces, and sufficient space to facilitate privacy for individual dyads.

Materials

I. Blank paper for each participant.

II. A pencil or pen for each participant.

Procedure

I. *(Five minutes.)* The trainer introduces the activity and its goals.

II. *(Ten minutes.)* After reviewing the material presented in Roles of the Process Politician in Chapter 2 of the guide, the trainer distributes blank paper and pencils or pens and then asks the participants to list the things they would do if each of them had a magic wand and could do anything desired regarding a specific group to which he or she currently belongs.

III. *(Fifteen minutes.)* The participants choose partners, share their lists, and help each other decide on one goal apiece to pursue within the next year.

IV. *(Ten minutes.)* The trainer instructs the participants to assist each other in determining and listing action steps directed toward achieving their goals. It is further stipulated that each participant include one step to be accomplished within the next six weeks.

V. *(Ten minutes.)* The total group is reconvened for a discussion during which the participants are invited to share their goals and action plans.

VI. *(Ten minutes.)* The activity is discussed and evaluated.

Variation

The participants may be asked to focus on work-related groups.